ME AND JAKE
by
Allan Young

ME AND JAKE

by Allan Young

Hunters and fishermen don't go hunting or fishing just to bring something home, anymore than a sports fan goes to a football or baseball game just to see his team win. With the latter it is all the excitement of being there. It is the color, the noise, the bands, the pretty girls, the hot dogs and beer, the thermos of coffee, the pre-game festivities and, usually, the big party afterwards. And of course, there is the companionship.

But the fan doesn't have to justify being there.

The hunter and fisherman does, though. He feels guilty if he doesn't bring something home—and the bigger it is or the more quantity it is, the better he can justify his going in the first place.

But that's not why he goes. He, too, goes for the color, the excitement, the companionship and the thermos of coffee. (Although there are damn few pretty girls!) His problem is that he can't just go and enjoy the fun—he thinks he has to come back and show what he got, or tell about what he almost got. Even the stuff the writers write has to contain the ultimate catch or kill of the object.

The fact is that the color of the mountain hardwoods in fall, or bright sun on blue water, really serve as food for the soul, and the idiotic things that happen to him and his friends keep the hunter or fisherman in a constant enjoyable frame of mind, with an ever-youthful attitude.

In a brief anecdote form, I have herein set down some of the most ridiculous happenings that have come my way so that you can see why hunting and fishing isn't all that serious a business. And I haven't even changed any names to protect the innocent!

THE BURYING AGREEMENT

Me and Jake long ago adopted the "golf adage" which says, "Anyone who mentions his job or business on the golf course has to buy a round of drinks when we get back to the clubhouse."

We had also adapted this slogan to other sports, including hunting and fishing. Who wants to be with someone who either gripes continuously about his job or tells all the juicy gossip at the plant or office—or perhaps is trying to sell you something—when you are out enjoying nature?

Then, as time went by, we invented another rule: "Whoever dies on a trout stream or in a duck blind or corn field will be buried where he falls."

The survivor is not going to suffer a heart attack or double hernia dragging the other big carcass out!

Then when I fell in a hole full of water on a duck hunting trip I had to hurry up and tell him he could not leave me there, because the agreement did not include burial at sea!

Later on a brilliant fall day, with the leaf color at its best in Fayette County, we were descending the bluffs to Bear Creek when the Moose stumbled and fell.

I turned to inquire if he was alright and he said, "I wouldn't tell you if I wasn't, because I'm sure you'd implement the burying agreement even if I was just crippled!"

He's right, I would!

DUCK HUNTING COWBOYS

Me and Jake turned out to be duck hunting cowboys. We drove into the farmyard on a cool spring day to be greeted with a scene normally reserved for a sale—cars, trucks and people all over the place. I inquired as to where the owner could be located, and someone pointed out a big burly man in coveralls.

This had all started when we decided that the river bottoms between Anamosa and Olin might be a good place to hunt ducks. We had discovered Muskrat Slough, a large shallow lake about a mile in diameter that made up a public shooting ground. (They even blew a bugle to signal shooting time!)

All the idiots and skybusters were there, so we didn't like to hunt there. But, since the Slough was only a few miles from the Wapsipinicon River, it stood to reason that when the "army" opened up on Muskrat, that the ducks would head for the river.

So, in taking a canoe down that twenty-mile stretch of river, on one of the trips we shared with our wives in summer, we found the ideal spot for a duck blind—an island in a place where the river was wide, and so was the surrounding open country. There were even a few potholes back in what timber there was.

Apparently the land on both sides of the river belonged to the same owner, so we set about finding him. Hence the Saturday morning trip to the farm about four miles away, to meet the owner.

Approaching him, and introducing me and Jake to him, I asked him for permission to hunt ducks on his stretch of the river.

Instead of answering that question, he said, "Can you boys handle a horse?"

We told him yes, we had both grown up with horses.

"What about cattle?"

We told him we had also grown up with cattle.

He said, "Good, we're about to drive over two-hundred head over to that place you are talking about, and we need all the help we can find to get them over there."

He told us to get ourselves some saddles out of the shed, and catch a couple of horses out in the barn lot. We found two old beat-up saddles, and threw them on a couple of harmless looking old stump suckers, still rough with their winter hair, adjusted the stirrups to our long legs, and climbed on board.

There were about a dozen of us, and some had to continually ride ahead to block off roads and lanes as we drove the herd along the back country gravel roads to the river. It was kind of fun playing cowboy, and it took us all morning to move the cattle the four miles.

When we had finished putting them through the gate into the river pasture, several women drove up in pickups and set out hot coffee, beer, pop and sandwiches—a welcome sight indeed!

We then rode our horses back to the farmhouse, unsaddled them, rubbed them down with a burlap sack, cleaned and oiled the saddles (something that hadn't been done in years, if ever) and again approached the boss farmer.

I said, "Well, what about it, can we hunt over there?"

He said, "I can't give you permission to hunt over there, because if I do, I'll have to let everybody hunt."

"We only hunt ducks," I told him, "and we are very careful of livestock and property."

"I'm sorry," he replied, "but I cannot give anyone permission to hunt in there!"

But he had a grin on his face and a gleam in his eye!

Taking the cue, I asked, "Will you run us out if you catch us in there?"

Again, "I said I can't give you permission."

This time without laughing.

Me and Jake built a blind on that island and hunted there off and on for seventeen years, and, since we missed his spring and fall cattle drives, never saw him again.

But you bet he knew when we were in there!

SKY SHOOTERS

I am sure you have seen and heard of many lucky, or just plain good, shots. There are several that I remember well.

One day we were standing there back to back in that island blind when suddenly Jake's gun went off in my ear. I wheeled around to see a lone mallard drake dropping from the sky.

I said, "Why didn't you say something?"

To which he replied, "There was only one!"

This was carried even further one year when Ray and Bob were hunting the river bottom ponds with us. (I'll tell you about Ray later!) A pair of woodies came whistling in on our end of the pond while I was pouring a cup of coffee.

Jake fired one shot and, since the ducks were side by side, both fell. Frankly, in all my years of hunting, that is the only double I have ever seen taken.

Bob and Ray yelled their congratulations from the other blind and I told them I didn't shoot because there were only two ducks, and since they came in on the Moose's end of the blind, and we always get doubles, I let him have them.

And those two nuts believed me!

Later that same day a lone Canadian honker came over, and since Ray didn't know what it was, he pointed up and shouted, Yo!"

The Moose said, "Yo, hell!" and bagged the goose.

Then "Yo" became a standard call with us.

The next morning two birds of undetermined species zipped in over Jake and me, so to have some fun, we shouted "Yo," and, with two shots from the other blind, two poor old pigeons fell dead on the water in front of us!

"What kind of ducks are those?" Ray asked.

We couldn't answer for laughing!

Once, on Lake Odessa, we were surrounded by sky shooters. A flock headed our way was flying high over the next blind boat when a single shot rang out.

"You can't hit anything that high, you stupid son of a ——-" shouted Jake. And then, "Nice shooting, fella!" as one duck came tumbling down.

CRAZY DUCK HUNTERS

You don't have to be crazy to hunt ducks, but it helps!

The first time I ever hunted ducks in the Lake Odessa region was late in the season, after the flight was really on. Me and Jake had planned to hunt our usual spot on the Wapsipinicon that weekend, but decided on Odessa instead. The idea was to go down the river in our boat and go in over the dike to the marshland after shooting time. No one was allowed in the hunting area before that.

So we put the boat in at Grandview at about one o'clock in the morning, and since it didn't take as long to get to the spot we had all staked out, we wound up with a long wait on a sandbar on the river side of the dike.

Moose said, "Let's build a fire and take a nap."

So, there we were, two idiot duck hunters trying to keep warm around an open fire on an icy twenty-degree winter night. I dozed off once, and while I was asleep he had worked his way around between me and the fire. I woke up with my legs so cold I could actually hit myself on the thigh and couldn't feel a thing!

Hours later, in a blind on a little pond, we really lambasted the ducks. Then, with me in the blind, and the Moose out in the brush hunting downed ducks, the conservation officer came up. After checking me, he asked if the guy out in the brush was with me. He also asked if we were the ones who had spent the night on the sandbar. When I answered yes to both questions, he just walked away. But not before giving me one of those looks that said, "Anybody as crazy as you guys has got to be legal. I won't even check that guy out in the brush!"

NEW SHOTGUN

The duck season had just opened in mid-October when me and Jake and our basketball coaching friend were entering a floating duck blind from a john boat. We didn't like taking visitors with us on hunting trips, but this guy had prevailed—wanting to learn the ropes. Instead of handing his new Browning automatic to one of us, Coach chose to crawl into the blind, gun in hand. When the boat moved a few inches away, as boats tend to do, he sought to balance himself by grabbing onto the blind. Down went the Browning into the Mississloppy!

I was hunting with an old Remington pump, and Jake with his father's ancient double—not much money between us for hunting equipment, so we envied Coach his new automatic.

After the early morning shooting died down, we began to feel sorry for Coach, who had sat there not participating. I told him we could go back home and get a grappling hook and try to retrieve his gun, but he said no, that he was all done with this sport forever—didn't ever want to see that Browning, or any other shotgun, again!

He asked if I would crank up the boat and take him over to the home of a friend on shore where he could call his wife to come and get him—he didn't want to ruin our hunt. After taking him all the way home, because there was no one at the friend's house, I rejoined Jake in the blind, and we finished out the day.

Several days later Old Moose and I were back in the same blind and he pulled a new Browning out of his gun case.

When I congratulated him on his acquisition, he just said, "Well, the price was right—too good to pass up."

"Yeah," I said, "just fifteen feet of cold water and some clean-up effort. Right?"

Old Jake just grinned!

CONSERVATION OFFICER

I know I said everything happens to me and Jake, but this isn't necessarily always true—sometimes it just happens to one of us. So I might as well tell you what happened to me one opening day of duck season, a Saturday when I had an appointment at the office.

I took my favorite Black Labrador, Dixie, and went to the river bottoms real early with the idea of getting some shooting from the railroad tracks. Legal shooting time was a few minutes after six.

At about five-forty another hunter came along and sat down by me, petting Dixie and engaging me in pleasant conversation.

At five-forty-five a flock of ducks flew over us.

I said, "It's tempting, but it's too early."

Other hunters in a blind further down the slough really cut loose on the flock.

This happened several times, and each time I remarked that the game warden must be around here somewhere, and he should get after those guys.

Eventually shooting time came, and my newfound friend and I got some ducks, which Dixie retrieved.

Then my friend said, "Can I see your license and duck stamp, please?"

And he flashed a badge!

That son-of-a-gun went on down below, and he was still writing tickets when I left for my appointment, a half hour later!

FIRST DOG

Old Jake had just gotten a new dog. She was a bit small for a Black Labrador Retriever, but at nine months of age she was partially trained by her former owner, a service station operator who decided to go back to college. At least the price was right—he gave her to Moose free.

Duck season, back then, used to open on Wednesday in Iowa (so all the doctors and lawyers could get first crack at them, I guess), but we used to take off work and go anyway. (I remember telling the boss that I would work sixteen hours a day for him all year, but opening day of duck season I would take off, even if he fired me. He never did.)

So, we took the dog, Ebby was her name, and headed for the Iowa River bottoms between Tama and Chelsea, as we still do on opening day. We were sitting back in the timber on a backwater when a whole flock of "malyards", as an old Mississippi river island buddy of ours from "Quinsey" calls them, came wheeling in over the trees. A beautiful sight, all brown and blue and white and green against the yellow leaves of the river bottom maples! After the initial opening day fever left us, there were four dead mallards on the water. Ebby, good dog, went off the bank in a streak of black, and all ducks were retrieved. It looked like a good day.

But later, as the shooting slowed, we hiked back to the car, about a mile, and started driving down the dirt road for another pond. About a half mile down the road we met Moose's brother-in-law, Bill, who had come to join us. Bill suggested another area back the other way, so we turned around and went back.

There, sitting along the roadside, where our car had been parked, was old Ebby. Moose had completely forgotten that he had a dog!

We hunted with that old dog for nine years, and she never forgot that day. Every time a car door was opened, Ebby would knock us down being the first one in!

THE DOG, THE COW, THE HAT

Another day in the life of Jake's dog was the time the cow ate his hat. It was late in the season of the first year he had Ebby, his first Black Lab. We were still hunting, although most of the ponds were frozen and the river had ice floes in it.

There was a timber pond across the river on the cattleman's place, which was really good for late season mallards if you took the time to break some of the ice on it. Since it was only about knee deep, this was easy enough to do. The problem was that it was on the wrong side of the Wapsipinicon River, and the river had to be waded to get to it. Fortunately there was a cattle crossing not too far away where the river could be waded with hip boots.

We came to the river and the Moose said, "Here, carry my gun."

I said, "What for?"

"I'm going to carry Ebby. I don't want her out in all that ice."

"You're kidding!"

So I carried the gun and he carried the dog.

When we got to the pond and started breaking the ice, here come old Ebby, jumping around and helping us!

Later, back at the river crossing on the way home, I didn't say anything—just reached for Moose's gun.

"Go to hell!" was all I could get out of him.

Oh yes, about the cow eating his hat. As we had approached the pond earlier, there was a flock of mallards working, so we crawled into a thicket for cover. In the act of getting in the bushes, Moose knocked his hat off, and didn't get back for it until the ducks were gone.

So was the hat. We couldn't find it anywhere. But there was an old red cow standing by the thicket placidly chewing her cud.

Even though no one believes it, especially me, the old Moose swears the cow was chewing on his hat!

RETRIEVERS

And now, Jake the retriever versus Ebby the retriever.

I'll never forget one day at Lake Odessa. We had built the ultimate in duck blind boats. It had everything but hot and cold running water—and on this particular day it had cold running water. There had been a storm the night before and it was full. Moose and I bailed it out in the dark with a garbage can and we shoved off.

Moose expertly guided the big boat (it was eight feet wide and eighteen feet long) through the channels and cutoffs toward the open water and found a nice spot to drop anchor.

The shooting was good, and soon we had dead ducks on the water. Jake, who wore chest waders, bailed out of the boat after the first volley, racing "Ebby" for the ducks.

Exasperated, he turned around and shouted, "I forgot about that damned dog!"

I said, "Come on back, Jake, she'll get the ducks!"

But next time we shot ducks, over the side he went again!

On the third time around, I swear to you, Ebby looked around at Jake to see what he was going to do!

DUCK HUNTERS' BREAKFAST

The Moose grew up around the Tama Indian settlement, and started hunting and fishing as soon as he was old enough to walk. He calls himself "The Old Indian Guide," and it used to upset him when I would tell people that he was half Indian.

Especially when I would say, "That's the front half. It isn't something that he inherited—it's just something that rubbed off."

Two brothers, Walt and Bill, are married to Jake's two sisters—and how those guys love the outdoors!

One of the first times they hunted ducks with us, or us with them, we were invited up to the home of one of them, I don't remember which one, for a late breakfast. We were tired, hungry and dirty from hunting—and sitting by each plate was a glass of brew that looked just like we did. I took a premature sip of mine very gingerly—and oh, brother, home-brew for breakfast!

Amid the smiles of the others, our hostess said, "You don't have to drink that stuff. How about some orange juice?"

Having learned a long time ago that making an ass of yourself is no way to prove your manhood, I said, quietly, "Anything at all, Ma'am, even water."

Soon the Moose and I started on our fifty mile journey home in his Buick Roadmaster. About five miles down the road he suddenly shuddered and gave out with an "Aaarrrgh!"

I said, "Want me to drive?"

"No, I feel alright. It's just the taste backing up on me."

After another five miles or so, he turned a very green face toward me and said, "Still want to drive?"

COLD AND WET

It's the natural state of the duck hunter, right?

Me and Jake hit Muskrat Slough one cold November day when the Northern Flight was on, and the ducks were really moving. There were times when just about all you had to do was stick your gun barrel up in the air and pull the trigger to get a duck.

There was only one other pair of hunters on the slough that day, and he and I had put up a temporary blind out in the water a ways, where it was about a foot deep. We were both wearing hip boots, and we had dragged a good sized log out in the water to sit on.

After the early morning shooting had died down, we were sitting back relaxed, enjoying our pipes and a couple of cups of coffee.

The Moose said, “You know, I never get cold around the butt, normally, but it’s so cold today that even that is chilled.”

“By George,” I said, “mine too. It’s as cold as a well digger’s in January.”

With that we both stood up. Our log seat had slowly and imperceptibly sunk into the mud so that we had both been sitting in about three inches of water! But the weather had been so cold that we had not noticed.

All we needed was a hungry gut, right?

COLD AND WET, AGAIN!

The island in the Wapsipinicon had been a favorite duck hunting spot of ours for years. Most of the time you could walk up to the back side of it in low rubber boots, the water was so shallow, while on the river side it was over your head. There were real neat places for decoys above and below the blind, and the island was situated in a bend in the river so that everything that flew that way passed right over it.

One day we went over there and the river was up, so that there was a lot of water behind the island. I had torn my hip boots and had left them home, expecting to walk out to the blind easily.

Jake said, "Come on, I'll carry you."

I said, "You're kidding."

"No, you carry both guns, and I'll just wade out to the island with you over my shoulder."

So he did—we both only weighed about two-hundred pounds back then.

When we came to the island, he proceeded to deposit me on a steep edge, and my feet proceeded to slip out from under me, and I proceeded to slide down the mud bank of the island to end up sitting in about eighteen inches of cold water!

My turn came about three years later, same place, same way—but I swear to you it was an accident!

Moose had lost a hip boot, and since he had acquired another retriever, just didn't bother to buy a new pair.

Again, the river came up. This time I volunteered to carry him. As we approached the island my feet got stuck in the mud and I couldn't move. As I thrashed around trying to get loose, his dog came over to see what we were doing. Just as I extracted one boot from the mud, she ran under it and in trying to regain my balance, I dropped Moose.

As I said, it was strictly accidental—but you can't get him to believe that!

AND AGAIN!

Me and Jake were hunting the river bottoms between Tama and Chelsea on cold November day when we both took a dip. First it was me. We were on our way out to go uptown and eat lunch when it happened. The bottoms were flooded from some late fall rains, so we had to wade in and out, for what seemed like miles. I simply stepped in a hole and went in over my boots.

In trying to extract one foot from the mud, I lost my balance and went in even further—clear to my waist!

Moose laughed, threatened to bury me there, then thought better of it and helped me out of the hole. Back in town I changed clothes. I had learned a long time ago to carry extras when hunting or fishing. But I had no other waders, just a pair of knee boots—and it would be a long time before my hip boots would be dry enough to put back on. And I did want to get in some evening shooting.

While having lunch with Jake's dad, the old man suggested we take his little john boat back with us. We could float down the river and get some shooting.

Jake said he had a better idea. Since he still had dry boots, he would walk through the marsh and pull the boat with me in it, until we reached one of our best spots.

This worked just fine, until we started home in the dark. Moose was tired and hungry, so he decided to take a shortcut across the marsh, instead of going back the way we had come.

I was sitting in the boat enjoying the ride, as he pulled me through the shallow water, when suddenly he disappeared from my line of sight. I jumped up on the front seat of the boat, to find him lying on his back in the cold water! The boat had caught on a grassy hummock and stopped its forward motion, jerking him backwards by the rope, which he had over his shoulder.

"Are we still burying at sea?" I inquired.

"Shut up and help me out," he growled. "I should have known better. Everything that happens to you eventually happens to me."

DECOY RETRIEVERS

At one time me and Jake had identical black Labrador retriever pups, seven months old, from the same litter. Oh, his was bigger than mine, but they still had the same lines and seemed to have the same intelligence. Both were females.

Since I lived near a lake, I had worked with mine all summer around the water. He had no such convenience. So, when we took them to the river bottoms on opening day of duck season, his was still a little inexperienced in water, although both were retrieving the scented dummies well.

We had two blinds on a large pond, and our intent was to put out decoys in front of each blind. Moose stopped off at the first blind with his dog, Belle, and a sack of decoys, while I continued on to the second with my dog, Dixie.

Of the first eight decoys I threw out, my dog brought back five—before she really believed I was mad! You should have heard the razzing from the other blind about my well-trained decoy retriever. Until I walked over and found that Moose had tied Belle to a tree!

Later on, when we had dead ducks on the water, I threw a mud clod out by one and yelled “Fetch!”

Both dogs swam out to the duck, sniffed it a couple of times, then each brought in a decoy!

Then, we finally had a duck fall on land. Moose threw it out a ways on the ground, and Belle would retrieve it every time. Dixie just sniffed it and walked away.

Then I threw it in the water and Dixie got the idea—and brought it in every time. But Belle wouldn’t enter the water.

So, we decided we had one good dog between us!

By the end of the day, though, they were both working well.

HUNTING WITH RAY

We had a hell of a time with Ray. He was from Long Guyland (as he pronounced it), and liked a shot of Vodker, (as he called it), once in awhile—but he had never hunted ducks.

I brought him into Iowa the day before opening day, where we met the Moose.

Now Ray was fat—not exactly obese, mind you—but good solid fat, probably about three hundred pounds.

He had no hunting gear, so before accepting our invitation to go, he went out and bought a new automatic shotgun, insulated hip boots, hunting pants, coat and hat. I think he invested more that one day in gear than the two of us had in our entire lives! He was ready, and it was really too bad what happened to him.

The early morning shooting was really good in Otter Creek Marsh in those days, before they civilized it, and we wouldn't miss it on opening day for the world. But Ray did.

We got a little worried when Ray climbed over the first farm gate. Now Jake and I are big, but we don't have trouble with farm gates. Or slogging through a foot of water and mud. But Ray did.

About a hundred yards into the marsh I heard a shout. Turning around, I could see only Ray's head and shoulders. He had stepped into a hole up to his armpits—all cold water!

And he had no other dry hunting clothes to put on.

I'll say one thing for him though. He insisted on sitting in the car alone while we got in on the early shooting. I offered to take him back to town but he wouldn't hear of it—wouldn't ruin it for us.

He got the last laugh that day, though. Two of them in fact!

After we got him uptown and dried off, and ran his clothes through a laundromat, we were back in the marsh in a makeshift temporary blind.

A Canadian honker came along straight overhead and Jake said, "Shoot him, Ray. You need a little target practice."

I still don't know if he deliberately planned it that way, but when that goose fell, it came directly at the Moose! As he dodged around trying to avoid it, his feet stuck in the mud and he lost his balance. As he went down he grabbed at something to sustain himself, and that something was me! As we both lay there, spread-eagled in about a foot of mud and water, Ray couldn't keep his laughter in—but then neither could we!

SWEETEST DAY AND RAY

The second year Ray went with us his wife was madder than hell! It never occurred to her that his duck hunting was not a one shot deal. Besides that, the day after he left was his son's birthday.

But, after all, he had invested in all that equipment the year before—and, since he had gotten ducks, he was now an enthusiastic duck hunter, and would be for the rest of his life.

As we drove out of town the day before the season opened, we passed a florist.

I said, “If my wife wasn’t speaking to me, I’d go in there and send her a dozen roses.”

Ray said, “I will! Turn around.”

Once inside, we saw a sign which said, “Tomorrow is Sweetest Day. Say it with flowers.”

Now, we had never heard of Sweetest Day, but it comes the third Saturday in October. It could be just another trick to sell gifts and flowers, but then again it might have been invented just to ease the consciences of duck hunters.

Anyway, it sounded like a good idea—so I, too, sent home a dozen roses, with an appropriate card.

The Moose, saving his money for more shells, I guess, decided that half a dozen was enough. But we found out later that the florist goofed up and put in seven by mistake.

Upon our arrival back home after a successful weekend of hunting, we dropped the Moose off first. As he was unloading his gear, his wife came out and expressed her appreciation for the “Sweetest Day” flowers.

“But why seven?” she asked.

“Er, ah,” stammered Jake, “one for each day of the week!”

He was always fast on his feet for a big man!

HUNTING WITH LARRY

Me and Jake have hunted together, usually just as a two-person team, most of our hunting lives, but we seem to draw all kinds of characters along with us sometimes. One of these was Larry. Now, you know you have to either be half nuts or have a ridiculous sense of humor to hunt ducks in the first place. And it helps if you have both attributes. Larry was just such a person.

When some guy invites himself along, it seems like the hunting is excellent his first time out, and he becomes a duck hunting nut. That's the way it was with me.

But, if you spend a lot of time trying to convince some friend of yours to try this great sport of shooting ducks, you can almost bet that neither of you will see a feather—let alone fire a shot.

On Larry's first time out it was the former.

He was a cowboy, steer wrestler, rodeo performer and judge—and an auctioneer. Showed up in a cowboy hat and carrying the world's rustiest shotgun. (Said he stored it under the couch in the basement.)

He really got the ducks on his first time out. So, his second time out was when his sense of humor had to be tested. That's an unwritten rule among duck hunters.

Like most second timers, he was all eyes and ears in the blind—ready for any sight of a duck. After the early morning shooting had died down, Larry sneaked back in the trees behind the blind about twenty feet to pour himself a cup of coffee. (I don't know why he left his thermos so far away.)

On a signal from me, Jake and I grabbed our guns and made like a flock of "malyards" was directly out in front.

Larry poured his coffee all over the ground!

(We have done that to guys who were eating a sandwich, lighting a pipe, taking a crap, picking up decoys or retrieving ducks. Of course it's been done to me, too.)

Then while we laughed (and he cussed us), a lone mallard dropped right over the blind. Larry was the only one with a gun in his hand so he threw it to his shoulder, and it clicked—no shell in the chamber!

SAVE YOUR SHELLS

Sometimes you don't even need to shoot, like the one time Jake got a goose at our Mississippi island blind. It was apparently shot on the Illinois side of the river about two miles away, and chose to fly over and drop among our decoys.

"It was a nice Canadian honker," said Moose, "but I wonder who shot it."

He kept it anyway.

The same thing happened to him again pheasant hunting, only it was a double. Four of us had just entered a field of standing corn to walk the rows, when a lone cock came down the row right at Jake. Just as he raised his gun it fell dead in front of him. When he went to pick it up there was another nearby—both still warm!

Back to the Big River blind again. We were standing watching thousands of ducks fly over and by—all out of range.

"Here ducky, ducky, ducky, ducky," I called. "C'mon down here and I'll shoot you in the fanny!"

"Still shootin' behind them, huh, Bear?" said Jake, in his most pitying voice.

THE BARE NAKED DUCK

Everything kept happening to me and Jake!

I had seen an ad in the newspaper about an old upright piano for sale, so we drove down to the farmhouse on the Iowa River to take a look at it. I thought it might go in my basement rec room for my kids to beat on. We figured that if I bought it, we could round up enough guys to move it later.

The old farmer, who had recently become a widower, was more than generous with a new bottle of Jack Daniels we had spotted on a kitchen shelf. By the time me and Jake were ready to leave, we could have rolled that piano end for end—so the three of us loaded it into my pickup and away we went.

As we drove out of the farmyard, I said, "Did you see that pond in back of his place?"

Looked more like a small lake, to me," said Jake. "You thinking what I'm thinking?"

"Yep," I said. "Let's go back before opening day."

So, with a bottle of Old Jack as a bribe, we got exclusive permission to hunt ducks on the best pond anywhere near that stretch of the Iowa River.

Opening day was excellent, as we lambasted the ducks from our hastily constructed blind, and so were many days following. But as the season wore on, and the shooting tapered off, we started jump shooting other small ponds and potholes on the place.

One day, while Moose was out checking potholes with the dog, a couple of mallards came over and I shot one, retrieved it and hung it up in the blind. Sitting there alone, smoking my pipe and sipping coffee out of my thermos, I absent mindedly started to dry pick the feathers out of the duck. I had most of the feathers removed from its body—you don't pick the head and wings, anyway—when another big flock flew in over the decoys. I jumped up and blasted away.

When the excitement was over, my picked duck was gone! I had thought it was dead, but apparently it was just stunned. I spotted it running down the sandbar along the edge of the pond and took off after it. You can imagine Jake's consternation, surprise and reaction when he came back to the bank overlooking the blind at this moment.

There I was, running down the sandbar, chasing a bare-naked duck, which couldn't fly (no tail feathers), and which would jump in the pond then jump out, shivering, and run some more.

"I would have given anything for a movie camera," the Moose said later.

THE TRUCK, THE POND

With apologies to a favorite country singer, I love pickup trucks! I don't know anybody that doesn't. I don't even want to know anybody that doesn't!

I remember reading once that the raw material in a car is worth only about twenty-one dollars before it is processed—untouched by human hands or machines. Some of my pickups were only worth that much, and I was driving them around!

As a kid, you always knew that if you stuck your thumb out in front of a pickup, you would get a ride. I have owned small ones, large ones, supercabs (my wife doesn't like those, too long), automatics, stick shifts, sun roofs, camper tops, flat beds, racks, four-wheel drives.

I have hauled grain, seed, lime, gravel, feed, fertilizer, furniture, stone, cross ties, fence posts, firewood, sawdust, manure, hay, corn, calves, colts, peaches, watermelons. I have towed stock trailers, camping trailers, boats and farm wagons.

I couldn't imagine myself without one.

I have buried them in mud, sawdust, manure, over a bluff. No one ever got hurt.

And then, me and Jake put one in a pond—it wasn't planned, it just happened.

Like I said earlier, what hasn't happened to us isn't worth mentioning, but maybe some of the things that did happen shouldn't be mentioned either!

Take that Thursday, for instance. We had downed three pheasants in a cornfield between New Sharon and Tama, when we decided to drive out along the Iowa River marshland between Tama and Chelsea to check out our old duck hunting spots. (All the ponds were frozen.) Jake was driving my pickup—claimed he knew the territory better than I did, having been born and raised there. All day long he had kept saying he wanted to buy the truck.

"I'll write you a check right now," he kept saying.

(The truck was worth at least twice what he offered, at that time, being new, and with a topper on it and all.)

We had just passed an intersection on a mud road, where I had tried to convince him to turn around—but he refused, saying he knew that country well. Soon we came to a familiar spot where the road was touched on either side by a frozen pond. They were small lakes, really. Next thing I knew we were sliding sideways—then right onto the ice on the left side of the road.

As the truck broke through the ice and slowly settled into about two feet of cold water, Jake looked over at me and said, "You want to drive!"

I said, "Write me that check first!"

WINTERTIME ON THE MISSISSIPPI

Recently, during an early winter cold snap followed by a blizzard here in the mid-west, I received a letter from a southern California friend. Included in the envelope was a full color picture of said friend standing in his green grassy yard, with blooming flowers in the background. A caption on the back of the photo said, "Sorry to hear about your weather."

I immediately had a color photo taken of myself sitting in front of one of the three fireplaces at the Bentonsport house, my shoes off, a drink in one hand and the other resting on the head of my dog, Dixie—a picture of pure contentment! The caption on this picture, which went with a Christmas card to the Californian, said, "Is that a lawnmower in the corner of the photo you sent me?"

Winter does come early sometimes—and the snowmobilers love it! Look at all the tracks in the roadside ditches, and the gatherings on Sunday afternoons. It's really a great sport for the snow addicts. Don't you feel sorry for those poor southern Californians?

Of course the boating enthusiasts and duck hunters hate to give up early, as they had to this year. In fact, Jake and I had planned a final hunting trip to Lake Odessa, near Wapello, for November 30, but everything was frozen up there—so we didn't go.

Much different from another year, when we went all the way to Keokuk on the river on December 16.

We kept a real nice floating blind straight out from the mouth of Devil's Creek near Ft. Madison. One Sunday towards the end of duck hunting season we went down there to find it gone—floated away. We searched for it but couldn't find it.

A couple of weeks later we were discussing where that blind could be when the Moose said, "Let's take my big boat and go look for it—I would like to take the boat out one more time, anyway."

So, on the blue cold day of December 16 we launched at Don's Riverview Marina and shoved off. We went all the way down the Iowa shore, searching with binoculars, to the dam at Keokuk, then we crossed over to the Illinois side and searched it on the way back. Still no blind.

How could a floating duck blind, about ten by twenty feet, of welded construction, just disappear?

Several hours later, cold and tired, we went into Don's to get warm. (Jake hardly ever puts the top up on his boat—and today was no exception.)

Don said, "What in the world are you guys doing on the river on a day like this?"

"Hunting a duck blind," we chattered.

"I wondered whose that was," said Don. "It floated upstream to the lower edge of Riverview Park, and I tied it up. You can see it from here."

That darn blind had really been blown upstream, and we had passed within one-hundred yards of it on the way down to Devil's Creek to start looking!

BOAT RETRIEVER

Jake had no business going up to our river blind by himself that Sunday morning, but he did anyway. We had planned to meet later that afternoon to put out the rest of our decoys—but, since he wasn't tied up, as I was, he went on up without me.

When I arrived, he said, "I don't have to tell you what happened to me this morning, but I will."

And here it is, in his own words.

"I came up too early because I got fouled up on the daylight savings time. But since I thought some other hunters might be up at the correct time, I decided to put in at my cousin's cabin and wait. It was still dark, so I had driven the boat up the river under a spotlight. I noticed that part of the dock was missing, so I ran the boat up on shore.

"Instead of running her further up on the bank, I had eased her up into the mud, grabbed a line and jumped out over the bow.

"As I jumped, I kicked the boat backwards away from shore and the wet line slipped out of my hand. So there I was, watching that big john boat drifting downstream about fifty feet out from shore. My gun and all my equipment were still in it—and so was my Labrador Retriever, sitting on the bow barking her head off.

"All I could think of was the ribbing I had to take that summer I lost my boat by getting it swamped in a storm—so, after about two minutes hesitation, I stripped to my shorts, plunged in the cold water and swam out to the boat.

"After bringing it back to shore, I went in the cabin, built a big wood fire in the stove, dried out my shorts, made a pot of coffee—got dressed and went on hunting. Got two big mallard drakes, too!"

He looked at me in consternation when my only comment was, "At five o'clock in the morning, in the dark, on an isolated chute in the river, why did you keep your shorts on?"

SNOWSTORM ON THE MISSISSIPPI

I had let the Moose talk me into getting an Illinois hunting license that year so we could hunt on the other side of the channel. We had put a blind in the stump field below Oquawka and the hunting had been excellent, although it was really tough picking your way through the stumps in a john boat.

We usually put in on the chute below our island, ran up the three miles to the island, then cut across the channel to the stump field, then went back in it another three miles. Also, to make the trip even more interesting, that was one of the widest channel crossings on the river.

On a warm summer day there is no more beautiful place on the river—lots of blue water and various shades of green foliage. It is also nice in the fall, with multi-hued yellows, reds and browns all up and down the water's edge, and in and out among the islands. But on a cold, gray winter's morning it can be very unappealing, and under certain circumstances, downright frightening.

All that fall we had made that run up and back two or three times each week, and had good hunting each time. Then, around December first, with the season almost over, we ignored the forecast of "a little snow" and went up there again. About mid-morning a few white flakes began to fall, which I pointed out to Jake.

"Must be some ducks overhead," he laughed, "and they are shedding their feathers."

Pretty soon it looked like all the ducks on the Mississloppy were shedding their feathers, and even Jake agreed that we had better make like two old hockey players and get the puck out of there.

Bucking an icy wind, we picked our way through the stump field very slowly, him handling the motor and me in the bow peering downward into the cold gray water and ahead into the impenetrable snow and waving directions back to him. I could hardly see him in the stern of the eighteen foot boat. Both our Black Labs were huddle in the bottom of the boat, keeping each other warm.

When we cleared the stumps I shouted back to the Moose to open her up, because all we needed was a set of barges as we crossed the channel. So, twisting the throttle wide open, he took aim by the seat of his pants and blasted full bore through the snow.

At about what I deemed to be three-fourths of the way between channel markers, my heart almost quit pumping as I heard a tow-boat horn—and close! Looking back, I saw the first barge, and then another, as their long, vertical rusty sides slid past Jake's end of the boat, just a few yards behind him. We were buried in the snowstorm's lack of visibility too much to see the others as we sprinted for the chute.

Later, Jake said he heard the horn but was afraid to look around. If we had been running just a few seconds later, we and our boat—and the dogs—would have been history!

And, you know, the Moose has never even mentioned getting an Illinois license since!

OVER THE DAM

Me and Jake have seen a lot of water go over the dam—and one day we went over it too!

It was a big Fourth of July celebration in Bonaparte—food, carnival rides, contests and a canoe race down from Bentonsport on the Des Moines River, where I owned a home, and our favorite of the old river towns.

We were fishing upstream several miles, in the backwaters, and since the river was extremely high, we decided to run down and check out the festivities. I was driving a little red and white fifteen foot runabout, which would really scoot along the smooth surface of the high water.

When we arrived on the river opposite the town, Jake asked, "Can you run the dam?"

I assured him we could on the south side of the river where the dam had washed out—especially with the water so high. As we went past the dam and slowed down below it, a young couple we knew waved to us, so we went over and invited them to join us for a boatride—which they were all too happy to do. After we made the pass up and down the river several times someone got the idea of putting in at the creek above the dam and going up to town and getting some lunch. This meant going back up through the washed out portion of the dam, then running across the river above it to enter the creek, where we could tie up and go eat.

About half way across the river, the gas tank on which we were running went empty. I looked around to the back seat and told the couple to switch tanks.

"What?" one of them, the man, asked.

I told him to just pull the one gas line loose from the motor and snap the other one on it.

"I don't know what you are talking about," he said, as the fast water took us backwards towards the dam.

"I'll go back and do it," said Moose.

"Better hang on, instead!" I shouted, and soon we were looking up at the dam from down below, in the tailwater. Fortunately, we did not capsize—but it was a lesson in boating. Make sure the occupants of your boat know a little something about what to do in an emergency.

Later, one of my neighbors said he and a friend were standing on the bridge, when the friend said, "Look at those idiots in that red boat going over the dam!"

My neighbor told me he said, "I hate to admit it, but I know those idiots!"

DOC'S BOAT

Me and Jake have long been aware of the humor involved in the medical profession. Maybe it has something to do with the types of personalities that are drawn to that kind of work, or perhaps after seeing people in all kinds of dire physical straits all day you have to develop a sense of humor to keep from going nuts.

And there is no one in the world with a drier sense of humor that Doc. And that brings us around to Doc's boat.

Rosemary and I had bought a large pleasure boat. We had spent quite a bit of time on tri-hulls belonging to friends, so we wouldn't settle for anything less. We hadn't much more than got it home when Doc and his wife came over to see it. Doc went down to Don's marina the next day, the way I heard it, and told Don he wanted one just like it. So Doc bought a nice shiny green two-tone tri-hull with a hundred horse motor.

Paul got to looking at it and so he traded his boat in on one just like it. Sonny traded his boat in on Paul's, then Rick bought Sonny's. If I had known Paul was going to trade, I would have preferred his boat in the first place, but if I hadn't bought mine, Doc might not have—then Paul might—oh, well, you get the picture.

Doc said that when he went down to resister his boat the girl at the courthouse asked him, "Do you have a toilet on your boat?"

Doc says, "I told her we carry a three pound coffee can—and she just went right on typing, didn't even look up!"

Now, Doc is an avid fisherman, and he is always out in those stump fields in the Missisloppy where angels fear to tread—but he does catch a lot of fish. (Of course his first prop only lasted a week!)

The following Sunday Rosemary and I were cruising up the river with Jake and Bettie when we spotted Doc's boat way over in a stump field on the Illinois side. Doc and his wife were both standing up waving their arms.

Jake said, "I'll bet old Doc's busted a prop, or knocked a hole in his boat, and is stranded."

So I gingerly edged our brand new boat and motor through the stump field, where we had been almost afraid to take a small flat bottomed john boat before, and pulled up alongside Doc's boat. Whereupon Doc said, "Hey, your boat is just like ours!"

And that was all he wanted!

FAST WATER AND COTTONMOUTHS

Me and Jake have always liked canoeing—especially when it was connected to fishing. We thought we were pretty good at it, and were never really afraid on the streams or lakes.

Neither of us were afraid of snakes, but we still gave them a wide berth—especially in cottonmouth moccasin country. Somebody once asked me how you can tell a cottonmouth from any other type of moccasin. I told them that the cottonmouths are the ones that run 'towards' you!

We canoe and fish several backwaters in which many logs and stumps are half submerged—and they are usually infested with moccasins, but no cottonmouths. Too far north and too cold for them. But we do fish southern streams where they are prevalent.

Recently we were on the Eleven Point river in Missouri fishing for trout in a big nineteen foot cargo canoe, when we ran some fast water which brought us close to a cliff. Jake had to really lay into his paddle against the rocks to keep us from being bashed against them. This brought my end of the canoe even closer to the cliff. What I saw made me almost turn the craft end for end!

"What's the matter?" shouted Moose, above the roar of the current, and I had to swallow my heart again before I could tell him.

As I had leaned my paddle against the cliff to push the canoe away, I found myself staring into the eyes and open mouth of the biggest cottonmouth I had ever seen—all coiled up on a ledge, about six inches from my face, and ready to strike!

'COON HUNTERS

Me and Jake had our 'coon hunting careers cut short by a hair-raising experience. Although both of our fathers were 'coon hunters, they had both gotten too old to climb the hills by the time we were big enough to be interested, so they had quit. But Jake's dad still had Old Joe around, and he liked to run—so one brilliant autumn moonlit night we decided to give it a try.

We didn't get any 'coons, but the old dog did tree once.

We could hear him barking down the slope a ways, so we started towards him. Soon we came to what seemed like a small cliff or outcropping of rock below us. After walking each way for a hundred feet or so, we decided that it must run the entire length of the slope. We could see the tops of some saplings five or six feet out from the edge of the cliff, so Moose suggested we jump into them and climb down. So, as he held the light for me, I dove headlong from the rock into a tree, grabbing on to a branch. Then I turned and held the light while he did the same.

Down we climbed—and down, and down. Soon we ran out of limbs, and the trunk was almost too big to reach around.

By the time we reached the ground, we had decided that our grove of "saplings" was a full grown tree reaching to the top of a seventy foot cliff!

Old Joe had lost his treed 'coon by then—so, two shaky amateur 'coon hunters went on home empty handed.

OLD JOE

Jake's dad has a collection of dogs as only he could have. When you drive up to his place you are liable to be greeted by two pekingese/terrier crossbreeds, a white hound with hemorrhoids, a nondescript long-haired Heinz-fifty-seven mixed female, and "Old Joe."

Old Joe is the star of the show. He is a little rickety when he walks, can't hear himself bark, and is a little absent minded, forgetting to come to eat sometimes. But you would too, if you were ninety-eight years old—because at fourteen, Joe is the equivalent of almost a hundred human years.

The old dog is a Blue Tick coonhound, which his owner raised from a pup, and who was his constant companion for many years. He came into this world with several strikes against him, being the only male in a litter of seven. Moose said it was a cold day when he was born, and Joe was so cold and stiff that they didn't think he was going to make it. So they took the pup in the house and gave him a shot of whiskey. That started him on a long and fruitful life.

Jake's dad said that once when he was in the hospital, the old dog missed him so much that he couldn't get along with anybody. Then the summer when he was twelve and the coon dog swimming races were held locally—and someone had the gall to suggest putting a life jacket on him—not only did Old Joe swim the pond three times, but he took second place in the contest!

Joe travels the surrounding country at will, and he knows where he can hop through or crawl under the fences, since he can't jump over them anymore.

But his real crowning glory came at the age of fourteen, when he became a father again—and of six pups, no less! Who knows, maybe Old Joe is just getting his second wind, and will be around for another fourteen years.

TROPHY PHEASANT

I never took my hunting and fishing seriously. It was something to do for fun, and, of course, I do like fish and most game to eat—especially if I cook it outdoors, even at home on the patio. But neither was I ever interested in trophies. But, however, I do have a good friend who has learned to stuff things, and occasionally he has wanted to do one for me at no cost.

After a day of pheasant hunting once, in which he participated, he insisted on mounting a rather large rooster, which I had bagged—so I let him.

Since he did have reasons to visit my office sometimes, I hung the bird on a paneled wall behind my desk. There it was, for all to see, in its ring-necked, wingspread beauty—in full flight, hanging from a wooden ring.

During the night someone took a piece of white paper about three feet square and ran over it with a car, so that a big black tire mark traversed the sheet from side to side. When we all came in the next day the paper was attached to the wall and the pheasant was hung over it. There, in all its glory, was a pheasant hit by a car!

Not knowing whether to laugh or cry, I just left it there—until my friend the taxidermist came in.

Talk about fire in a man's eye! If he could have found the culprit, I'm positive his hide would have decorated that paneled wall! Then he started to see the humor in it.

From then on I noticed the whimsy he was adding to his mountings—and he seemed to be enjoying his hobby more.

PREACHER'S PHEASANT

We were pheasant hunting with two of Moose's neighbors. The father of one of them owned a farm about thirty miles away, and we had been invited up for an exclusive hunt one day.

When we got there, the local preacher was visiting, and the old man suggested that he go with us. So they dug up an old rusty single barrel twelve for him, and away we went.

Now it was cold. We were wading slough grass and icy bogs all afternoon. The preacher was well dressed for it—in a ball cap and canvas shoes! I think his jacket was made of chicken skin, or something just as translucent. He didn't complain, though. He didn't shoot anything either—in fact, he didn't even take his gun off his shoulder—but he didn't complain.

At the end of the afternoon we had eleven pheasants—and Jake and I had seven of them. We had shot three apiece, and we had shared one. Oh, had we ever shared one! (I'll bet that if you laid it on a screen, it would have gone right through!)

Anyway, when we got back to the farmhouse, the old man suggested that since there were five families represented we take two birds apiece—and that he would take one.

As Moose and I were taking the birds out of the trunk of the car, he muttered, "I sure hate to give that preacher any of my birds. That S.O.B. didn't contribute anything to this hunting trip."

"Aw, quit complaining," I said. "Just be glad we didn't tell him about the 'no talking business' rule. The way you have been cussing him, he might say you were bringing up his business, and make you buy drinks. As for the birds, you can't keep them all—and besides, I know one bird we will definitely give him!"

"You mean the one that would go through a sieve?"

"That's the one, pal. Here, you hold this newspaper while I scoop the bird onto it."

So, we went home happy, and the preacher was happy that he had gotten two pheasants. At least until he got home and tried to clean them!

CLEAN BIRD

While we are on the subject of pheasants, you will find this story hard to believe, or maybe not.

A new young couple moved in right across the road from the Moose. City slickers, I guess, if there is any such thing anymore. Anyway, she found out Jake hunted pheasants, and kept telling him how badly she wanted to fix one.

So one Sunday afternoon Jake returned from hunting and presented her with a nice plump bird.

A few days later he asked her how they enjoyed their first pheasant.

"You didn't tell me they stink," said she.

"Stink?" asked Jake.

"Yes, stink," she said. "I tried roasting it in the oven, and when I took it out, it smelled so bad we couldn't eat it. I threw it out with the garbage."

Jake said, "You did get it good and clean, didn't you?"

"Oh, yes, we picked it real clean, just like my mother used to do a chicken."

"What about its insides?" asked the Moose.

"Insides? What insides?"

WHOSE SON ARE YOU?

It was the best hundred and twenty acres of pheasant hunting anywhere—slough grass along a stream down the middle, with corn on both sides—and it belonged to Jake's uncle.

That opening day, Moose's cousin was home on leave from the Army and decided to join us.

As we approached the far fence in our first pass across the field—bagging a few birds—some hunters came out of the road and started yelling at me, since I was closest to them.

"Get out of here," one screamed, "I don't allow anyone to hunt in here!"

"Just who are you?" I asked.

To which he replied, "This is my property, so get off!"

I called to Jake's cousin, who was farthest away, to come over.

"I just wanted you to meet your new father," I said. And turning to the slob hunter, "His father owns this property, so he must be your son."

"Well, I tried," said the idiot, sheepishly, as he and his buddies headed for their car.

GETTING PERMISSION

Me and Jake had flown over the place, up above walker, several times, and thought it looked like an upland game hunter's paradise. A couple hundred acres at least, and all obviously in a government set-aside program—what some laughing called "Jackie's Acres" during the Kennedy administration, or named them after whoever happened to be the President's wife since then.

We decided to find the owner. Luckily he lived on the place—in a big old two-story run-down farmhouse reminiscent of the "Peter Tumbledown" cartoons we had seen in our newspapers when we were young.

When we drove into his farmyard, he was sitting on the dilapidated steps of the front porch petting a large dog. Several other dogs were lying or standing around the place.

"I think it's your turn," I said to Moose.

We had long ago adopted the policy of taking turns in asking for permission to hunt or fish on private property.

Jake got about twenty feet from my truck and the old man said, "Sic 'em," to the dogs.

The whole mob came tearing at my partner, barking and growling their displeasure at his presence. I pushed the door open on his side and he dove headlong into the seat. I started the motor.

"Wait a minute, boys," called the old man.

Then he chased the dogs away and walked over to the truck.

"I was just having fun," he said. "You boys want to hunt here?"

"Well, yeah," I said. "We had planned to ask for permission, but we don't want to get eat up."

"You got it," he said, "and don't worry about the dogs. They're a bunch of pussy cats. I just use them to scare off people who invade my place without asking. In fact, you two are the first ones this year to ask. Come on in and have a cold drink, and hunt anytime. If you drive a different car sometime, just let me know—so I won't sic the dogs on you again."

We hunted there for years, and became very good friends with the old man—and the dogs!

JAKE'S HOLDING PEN

Me and Jake pretended to be farmers for awhile. I raised horses. But not him—he raised hogs! I used to tell him anything but hogs. Horse manure doesn't smell all that bad—good fertilizer for the garden. Cow manure I can tolerate. But hog manure, with that acidic smell, is repulsive. Of course he just said it smelled like money to him!

Because we hunted so much on other people's land, with permission, of course, we would let anybody hunt on ours—if they asked for permission. If they don't —.

One day I stopped to see him about some business, and he was studying his property some distance away with binoculars.

"What's up?" I asked.

"Some guys are hunting across the road without permission," he answered. "Come on."

I got in his truck with him and he drove to one of his hog holding pens. Taking a shovel out of the truck bed, he proceeded to scoop up a pile of wet, juicy, smelly manure and set the shovel gingerly back in the truck bed.

We drove to the interloper's car, Jake opened the door and tossed his load into the front seat.

Laughing, I asked, "What if the door had been locked?"

"I'd have broken a window."

Some unhappy landowners put sand in the radiator or gas tank, but he's too nice to do permanent damage.

I said, "What are the chances of those guys coming back and doing something destructive?"

"Oh, they'll be back," said Moose. "But after they tell what happened in town, somebody will tell them what the rules are, and they will ask permission next time."

RABBIT CHASERS

In Iowa, during a recent twelve-year period, 1.9 million hunters have killed 21.6 million rabbits, according to the Iowa Conservationist magazine.

Since me and Jake were out on a day on which three cottontails were bagged, we are well on the way to the next twelve years, with only 21, 599, 997 rabbits to go. And I got all three!

But I must admit, though, that I gave Jake his chance. He and I were walking down one side of a brushy draw, when we came to a secondary draw, which ran for about a hundred yards at right angles to the one we were following. I told the Moose that I was going to do him a favor and cut across to the head of the short draw and herd the game down towards him.

It didn't work. I kicked up one measly cottontail and, let me tell you, I shot behind that rabbit three times in order to chase it down to Jake, and he still didn't get it!

CHICAGO RABBIT HUNTERS

Remember what I said about giving permission to hunt on my place to anybody that asked?

The sound of barking dogs drew me away from the warm fire at the Bentonsport place and out into the yard. There in the driveway in the closing dusk sat a nondescript green beat-up old Ford station wagon, with a large wooden box tied on the top rack.

Getting out of the front seat was a skinny little dark skinned man, grinning from ear to ear. He asked if I was the new owner, and upon being told that I was, asked if they could hunt rabbits there. He then told me that there were six of them, from the south side of Chicago, and, with my predecessor's permission, they came there every year for two days of hunting—nothing but rabbits. They stayed at the hotel in Keosauqua.

When I asked about the contents of the box, he said, "Beagles, eight of them."

Early the next morning I heard them banging around up in the hills, while the dogs would occasionally howl as only a Beagle can. When the shooting stopped, and I presumed they had come down to their car to eat their lunches, I rode my horse up there. I was looking at the skinniest bunch of dogs I had ever seen—all their ribs were easily discernible, right through their skin!

I asked them how the hunting was, and they said they had gotten only half as many rabbits that morning as they had the first morning last year.

"And how many is that?" I asked.

"Just thirty-six," I was told.

"You mean you got seventy-two rabbits in just one morning? What do you do with them all?"

"Oh, it's a regular thing every year. We take them home, have a big feast, then share them with our friends and relatives. We only hunt these two days, and with no limit in this state, usually get over two-hundred rabbits."

They came back every year, for many years, and it was always the same—skinny guys, bony Beagles, old Ford wagon, box on top, and dozens of rabbits.

Talk about meat hunters!

BRUTUS AND THE QUAIL

There are quail, rabbits, turkeys and deer on the backside of our Bentonsport place, where the big spring and all the ravines are located—and I think most of them die of old age, since nobody hunts them. Remember, I am basically a duck hunter.

Just when I thought I was all through raising horse because all three kids had grown up and moved away, my oldest daughter sent me four quarter horses down from Wyoming to keep "temporarily." One of them was a big sorrel gelding which no one could do anything with, but I was determined he would earn his keep—so by hook or crook, and with a lucky break or two and some help from Jake, we became friends, and I rode him at will.

Moose would come down and we would trail ride up in the ravine country just for kicks, and the old gelding seemed to enjoy it just as much as we did. He had an Indian name that meant "The Wind," but I called him Brutus.

The turkeys came down and ate horse feed, and the deer were always licking the salt blocks, so the horses got used to them.

Then one sunny Saturday in the fall I was riding Brutus and Jake was riding Buck, a big buckskin more to his size, when we decided to make a pass high up through the hills just to look at the view. As we separated the two horses to ride around a stand of colorful oaks and hickories, I walked Brutus right into the middle of a large covey of quail! They went up on all sides, and he went straight up in the middle. Caught off guard, I kept going. There is no worse feeling than being fifteen feet in the air, all spread-eagled, with no horse under you. Fortunately, the ground was soft and grassy, rather than hard and rocky.

Old Brutus ran off a little way and waited for me, and Jake said the horse was looking back as if to say, "What are you wallering around down there on the ground for?"

FIVE-BELOW-ZERO BUCK

Although basically me and Jake are duck hunters, we will try something else once in a while. Like deer. I have never hunted deer. I don't know why, I just never had any interest. But Jake did, at least once. He even tried bear hunting once, joining an expedition to Canada. I needled him about that—he didn't get a bear, but he got a picture of a guy that got one!

But back to his deer hunt.

It was five below zero that morning, and the Moose was in a tree in the Iowa River bottoms right over an active deer trail in the snow. A few minutes after climbing the tree, he had a nice seven-point buck dead on the ground. After field dressing the deer, he attached it to a harness he had brought along, and started dragging it towards his pickup, about a half-mile away.

Now, the river is so crooked in that area that it is easy for a native to get lost—much less a stranger. And Jake was no stranger. So, Jake dragged his deer. And he dragged it. And he continued to drag it. He had parked his truck right in the edge of the woods, so it should be easy to find. Besides, who needs a compass in Iowa?

Several hours later, he broke out into an open field and looked around for his truck. He spotted it about two miles back! He had been dragging the deer parallel to the edge of the woods, and had passed within a hundred yards of his truck, and kept on going!

JAKE'S TURKEY

Jim, Jake's youngest son, has an excellent place to hunt turkeys down in Van Buren County on a friend's place. He met the guy a long way from home when the guy had car trouble and Jim helped him out—so they became fast friends.

Jim and some others talked the old Moose into going with them one fall. I don't know what it is about your kids, but as soon as they get past twenty they think you are senile, no matter what your age and condition. And that is the approach Jim was taking on Jake that day—they were really worried about something happening to him.

So they took him out in the turkey woods and sat him under a tree, with instructions not to move—the turkeys would be along near him later.

Let Jake tell it in his own words.

"I sat there for what seemed like hours, and, even though I could hear the boys calling turkeys further away, I was bored stiff.

"After awhile I got thirsty, and seeing no activity, and knowing the car wasn't far away, I decided to walk back to it and get a cold drink of water or pop.

"I came out to the road about fifty yards from the car, and, as I laid down on my stomach to slide under the fence, pushing my gun ahead of me, here come a big tom turkey trotting down the ditch. Immediately he belonged to me.

"Shortly thereafter, while I was congratulating myself, Jim and the others, having heard the shot, came up at a pretty fast clip and started chewing me out for moving. They had worked back around to my tree, and not finding me there, had feared the worst and started looking for me.

"I said, 'Hey, look at my turkey!' They didn't even look. Just kept telling me how I could have a heart attack, could have broken a leg or could have shot myself. I tried to tell them they knew I had done this all my life, and how about my turkey?

"And you know, those worrisome boys weren't the least bit interested in my successful hunt—just my health.

"I told them there was no sense in all of us worrying about my health—so while they stood there and worried, if that was what they wanted to do, I was going back in the woods for another turkey!"

SEA SICKNESS, OR NOT

We met in downtown Los Angeles for a big breakfast of potatoes, eggs, sausage and toast at four in the morning, boarded a friend's boat at San Pedro harbor at six, had corned beef and bloody marys at ten, and by noon I was sick to death!

I have never been seasick in my life. In fact, any kind of motion sickness is foreign to my system. I was in the Navy—rode out two hurricanes at sea. I have owned and driven every kind of boat imaginable. I am a licensed marine pilot and marine engineer, and hold a Master's License for inland lakes and rivers. I have flown airplanes upside down, and will ride any ride at the carnival or amusement park.

But that day I was sick. Of course, those Californians put more tabasco sauce in their bloody marys than you can imagine, and I do really like corned beef, so I tend to over indulge in it. It must have been that!

The captain/owner of the boat kept asking if I wanted to go back in, and I kept telling him that I would die out there first!

We did catch fish, but the climax came when Jake hooked something with dorsal fins, which the captain said was a sand shark. Harmless, he said.

Moose finally got it up alongside, and the captain expressed his disappointment when the twelve-foot monster got off the hook.

"I don't know," said Jake. "I wasn't too crazy about being in a boat with anything like that. And I wouldn't get out, because I don't know what else might be lurking in there waiting for a big overweight fisherman!"

BIG FISH

Personally I have never caught a really big fish. But I have been with them that have.

Back when my business used to take me to southern California several times a year I would always take an afternoon off and go out on a sport fishing boat in the blue pacific. In fact, for years I kept a fishing outfit hidden at a friend's place in the wilds of Burbank awaiting my repeated returns.

We always made up a pool on the boat for the biggest fish caught. I never won it. But others thought I did—at least once.

The first time the Moose accompanied me out there on a business trip he won it. But nobody knew but us.

The skipper of the boat told us to rig for bonito, because they were running. The very first strike on the boat was on Jake's line. Now, a large bonito is something like having a tiger by the tail. Their bones must be coil springs. That fish dragged Moose down the starboard side, across the stern, and halfway up the port side before he got control of it.

Later, as we were enjoying a sandwich on the way back in to the harbor, I said, "Moose, they are weighing in the fish, back on the fantail, and yours should win the pot."

He said he didn't think so, whereupon I took the big bonito out of the sack, took it back and had it weighed, collected the money, accepted everyone's congratulations as if I had caught it, tipped the boat boy out of the prize money, and didn't turn the rest over to the Moose until we were in our rental car and far from the wharf!

"You were being a little generous with my money, weren't you?" he asked.

"Since when did you get so bashful," I said. "I think I should have taken the cost of my fishing trip out of it, too."

The next time I left for the west coast, he said, "Who are you taking to catch the big ones for you this time?"

I don't get no respect!

FIRST ON THE LAKE

"Well, you're first," said the bait shop owner as we walked in. It was a cold March 9 afternoon, and he had just opened—just got his first load of minnows in, he told us.

Jake and I both had a bad case of cabin fever, so I had brought my boat and he brought his foldout camping trailer to Lake Rathbun to fish for early crappies.

We spotted the trailer in the unopened state park, launched the boat and proceeded to fish for the rest of the afternoon. Aside from catching only two little measly crappies, the day was uneventful until we found ourselves hung up on a log when we decided to give it up. It was well after dark by the time we bounced the boat around to clear the obstruction.

"How about some hamburgers and hot coffee?" said Jake, as we arrived back at the trailer—alone on the whole lake.

The gas stove wouldn't light! So, with a lantern, we went out in the cold and checked the bottled gas tank—plenty of gas. So we crawled under the trailer on the cold ground and started tracing the gas line—it was O.K. up to where it entered the trailer. Raising up the stove and sink unit, we found a flexible gas line wedged shut underneath—when the unit was folded over for use, it had flattened the soft line.

The hot coffee warmed us up, and the hamburgers filled us up. By now it was quite cold. The old Moose assured me that with a portable gas heater he had borrowed from his dad we would sleep warm. So, we lit the heater and climbed into the two outboard bunks, sleeping bags, insulated coveralls, thermo underwear, insulated socks and all.

In the wee small hours of the morning I woke freezing to death.

I kept thinking, "Why are we sleeping out here in these two bunks suspended in air, with only canvas over us, like it was summer, when we could be sleeping down by that heater on the couch and breakfast nook which made beds?

I heard Jake move, so asked if he was awake.

"You know we could be sleeping down by that heater," I said.

"I thought of that," he said, "But it's out of gas! Let's light the stove and cook breakfast. That'll warm us up."

"Let me know when it's ready," I said.

Daylight found us breaking skim ice off Honey Creek inlet in order to eventually catch some more little measly crappies.

When we finally got hungry enough for lunch, I nosed the boat up on shore and against my warning, the old Moose grabbed a line and jumped to shore. His feet slipped and he immediately fell backwards into the lake. The boat started to drift away, with me still in it. I nosed it up on shore again, and, wearing hip boots for just such an occasion, I stepped out. The wind swung the boat broadside to me, and in attempting to recover it, it pulled me in over my boots.

Looking over at the Moose, sitting disgustedly in the weeds, I said, "Anytime you want to go home!"

"Right now," he said.

BEFORE THE WIND

Thursday was a good day at Lake Rathbun—for us crappie fishermen, that is.

Moose's brother-in-law used to be the sheriff in Little Rock, and he had a home on Nimrod Lake, about fifty miles from there. A few years ago we joined him on a fishing expedition there for several days while the lake was up about ten or twelve feet. We were catching crappies so big that the Arkies choose to call them "saddle blankets" or "slabs."

So when we heard that Rathbun was up a similar amount, we knew it was going to be a good day.

Jake had a fourteen-foot deep vee fishing boat and a five-horse motor, such as it was, so we took that, knowing that my big boat would never take us where we wanted to go. The object, under all these circumstances, is to ease back up in the inlets among the trees and bushes, preferably over a creek bed. That's where the crappies are when the water is high.

We put in at the state park ramp and motored straight across that area of the lake to a small inlet, actually passing over a submerged pasture field fence. There we tied into what turned out to be a whole herd of slab crappies. I cleaned and brought home fourteen, but we must have thrown back three time that many.

After we got tired of catching them, we decided to go exploring, so we ran in and out of inlets until, guess what, we ran out of gas!

So the two old Indian guides took a sight on the spur at the state park, checked out the wind down the lake, and decided that with a little luck we would drift right to the boat ramp. It worked, too. We only had to row about fifty feet!

And we caught several more crappies and a couple of walleyes as we drifted.

CRAPPIETHON

They started holding a Crappiethon at the lake every year, and me and Jake would enter. We never won, but once we were still in the running until very late in the day. It's tough to compete against hundreds of teams, even on your own lake.

The first time we competed, we caught only sixteen fish, and none of them were very big. The contest paid twenty places, for the heaviest twenty fish. That first time we were really disgusted with ourselves, especially when we went back two days later and caught forty-one crappies, any twenty of which would have won!

LADIES' DAY

Me and Jake had taken our families to Lake Rathbun for swimming and skiing that first summer when it opened up, but had not been fishing with them. In September we went fishing there for the first time with our wives. Rosemary and I met Jake and Bettie one Thursday after the kids were back in school. It was too cold to swim, so we picked up minnows at the marina on the north side of the lake and went crappie fishing.

We went way back up in an inlet and tied up to some buck brush that was sticking out of the water about two or three feet. The water was six to eight feet deep. Being nice guys (?) we baited our fly rods with those "slippery slimy" minnows for the gals to use, and before we could get our own poles rigged there was a "whoops" from the bow of the boat, Rosemary, and another "whoops" from the stern, Bettie, as they each hooked a crappie simultaneously.

"Whoops" became the cry of the day, as they proceeded to catch one crappie after another. About the time it warmed up enough to go skiing, and the ladies were tired of catching fish anyway, a conservation officer pulled up alongside our boat.

"I'll bet you came to tell us where the people are catching all the fish, didn't you?" Moose asked.

"Well, I am making a survey of who is fishing and what they are catching," he answered.

In answer to his questions, we told him that we had been there about two hours and had caught over sixty crappies—mostly caught by the girls—and that we had also caught and released two walleyes and a largemouth bass.

He asked if we fished there often, and we told him yes, that on the last trip the two of us had taken home twenty crappies for a fish fry, but had released about three times that many. Three or four twenty to twenty-four inch walleyes were not uncommon to us.

So he said, "And you want me to tell you where the fish are?"

EVERBODY HAS TROUBLE ON THE LAKE

The next time our wives went with us turned out to be "one of those days."

Rathbun is a great sailing lake, and there are some great sailors on it—and some who are not so great. Me and Jake went down early to fish in the morning. Along about ten o'clock we headed for our favorite crappie cove, after fishing several inlets.

Strung across the cove were about a dozen large sailboats. We saw them all the time, especially on weekends. Sailors who never saw their sails, and probably didn't know what to do with them, anyway. They went down to the marina, boarded their boats, fired up their kicker motor, pushed the boat across the lake into a cove or inlet, partied all weekend, fired up the motor, and "sailed" back to the marina to their berth. No sails were ever raised.

As we cruised under the line which tied the string of boats to a tree, some guy came out of a cabin and started yelling to us to stay out, that was their cove. We gave him a "Hawaiian Salute" and went on back in the cove. When we came out later, there were a series of lines strung between the end boats on either side and trees on shore. We presumed to keep people like us out.

"You still got that hatchet in your toolbox?" asked Jake.

"In the bow, under the middle seat."

I eased the boat up to the lines on one side, and the old Moose had a good time cutting them with the hatchet, while all kinds of threats were called to us from the decks of several boats.

"Should we report it to the Corps of Engineers?" I asked.

"Hell, no!" said Moose. "Just keep that hatchet handy."

Me and Jake were sitting on a picnic table at the marina later, waiting for Rosemary and Bettie to join us, since they didn't want to fish all day, and we had already been out for several hours. The typical middle-aged couple came down to launch their boat, in a typical middle age fashion—she was backing the trailer in the water, while he sat in the boat ready to start the motor and back the boat off the trailer.

If I talked to Rosemary the way he talked to her I would probably be on the wrong side of the grass by now. He kept calling her “Dummy” and “Stupid,” telling her she couldn’t do anything right. We thought she was doing pretty well. Soon he backed the boat into the lake and she drove their car up on the hill to park. The lot was full, so she had to go quite a distance to do so.

Jake said, “Look at that S.O.B. I think he is in trouble.”

The man was running the boat around in circles at a high rate of speed and was waving his arms and shouting to get his wife’s attention. She was casually strolling down the driveway looking at the scenery and other boats.

As she neared our perch, I said, “Ma’am, I think your husband forgot to put the plug in the boat, and he wants you to go get the trailer, so he can put the boat back on it. That’s why he is running around in circles, to keep the water from coming in. If he stops, the boat will sink.”

And you know, that woman stood there for what seemed like several minutes deciding whether or not to go get the trailer!

That was the day we decided to keep a bunch of fish, so we could have a big crappie feast for our friends. My tri-hull, which we had opted to use in deference to the ladies, did not have a live well, so we kept our catch in a wire basket hanging over the side when we were not moving.

About three dozen crappies later, we headed for the marina. While I went to get the trailer, Moose prepared the boat for retrieval. He had set the fish basket in the shallow water beside the boat ramp. When I picked it up later, to go over to the fish cleaning station, it contained only five fish!

He had put the basket down over a rock, and since the bottom door in it had not been fastened, the rock pushed it open, and the fish swam away! So much for the fish fry!

But the day wasn’t over yet. As we drove home late in the evening, we came across a car stopped by the side of the road, and a wrecked john boat in the ditch back a little way from it. It was the couple with the plug problem.

She was sitting quietly on the back bumper of the car, while he ranted and raved about her not noticing that he had not clamped the trailer tongue down on the ball of the hitch. The boat had simply come loose from the car.

"Looks like she forgot to tell you to hook the safety chains, too," said Moose, winking at the woman—as we dragged the boat up the embankment and attached everything as it should have been.

"I'll bet that ends their fishing together," I said.

"If it was me, it would probably end us ever doing anything together," said Moose, while Bettie smiled in agreement.

YOUR BOAT, OUR BOAT

Me and Jake had a little old Cessna airplane, which was supposed to be a four-place, but with him and me at over five hundred pounds, it was a two-place—especially with all our fishing gear in it, too.

One nice spring day we flew it to Minnesota to go walleye fishing below lock and dam number three on the Mississippi. There is a gravel road that runs all the way from our home airstrip to Redwing. We always followed this road. "IFR" means "I Fly Roads," not "Instrument Flight Rules," as some people suspect! Two of our friends were going to drive up a day early and meet us there.

They picked us up at the little airport and we stopped for groceries on the way to the cabin on the river. It was dark when we got there, but no one mentioned supper—they just flopped down in front of the TV set and started drinking beer instead.

I went out in the kitchen, peeled some potatoes, fried them, plus a bunch of pork chops, made a salad and coffee, opened and heated a can of corn, and yelled, "Come and get it!

They all ate like pigs, got their coffee and headed back to the television. I started clearing the table and washing dishes and Jake came to help.

Four a.m. found me up and in the kitchen again, and with the old Moose's help, making up a bunch of "fisherman's special," toast and coffee. Again, after everyone ate like there was no tomorrow, me and Jake did the dishes, leaving the kitchen spotless.

When we walked out on the sandbar in front of the cabin later, I observed two john boats pulled up on shore—one about sixteen feet long with a twenty-five horse motor, and the other a twenty footer with a sixty-five horse. The big one had fishing tackle in it.

I called to Jake, and we started taking the tackle out and putting it in the smaller boat, then putting our tackle in the big one.

The other guys came running out, coffee cups in hand, yelling, "Hey, that's our boat!"

"That was your boat," I said, laughing. "It's ours now, and will be as long as we're cooking!"

Needless to say, it was our boat all weekend.

ALPINE INN

The Alpine Inn in Elkader was a stagecoach stop over a hundred years ago, and it hasn't changed much.

When me and Jake went north to fish for trout in a cold February week, we decided to spend a couple of nights there—right in the middle of our fishing area. It was certainly too cold to camp out, anyway.

We thoroughly enjoyed the warmth, hospitality, food and especially the rathskeller underneath it in the evening. Even the fact that the fire escape was outside our room, and in such an emergency, the guests would have broken our glass door and trooped across Jake's bed to get out, didn't bother us too much.

But Jake who owned newspapers, didn't have to write what he did about me in his sports columns!

"Here he was," he wrote, "a man who has traveled all over the world, walking through the lobby of the best hotel in northeast Iowa carrying on his shoulder an extremely large cardboard toilet tissue box full of clothes. You would think that such a man would be able to afford better luggage!"

Well, it's the only thing I could find that would hold a pair of chest waders, insulated coveralls, thermo underwear, storm coat and hat, a wicker creel, a fishing vest and assorted canteens and coffee thermoses!

BOOT BASS ON THE VOLGA

Me and Jake were camped on the Volga River near Fayette. Our former pasture field campsite is a golf course now, darn it! The world is just becoming too civilized. But back then it was a great place to camp, near that big spring and all. And the smallmouth bass were just waiting for your lure.

We had acquired hammock tents to simplify our camping—you know, the kind that is to be slung between two trees. It has a rainproof top and mosquito netting sides, with a zipper clear down one side so you can get in and out easily. Comfortable, but cold on a chilly night.

Now Jake didn't like to sleep between two trees, so he always put his hammock on the ground with his sleeping bag inside, and the top propped up on sticks. This particular night we had our tents about fifteen feet apart with a fire between us—it was cold!

I woke up to a cold foggy dawn lying on my side facing Jake's tent. I opened my eyes to see the face of a cow about six inches from mine. It startled me so that I jumped slightly. This frightened the cow so that she snorted, then wheeled, and ran right through the still sleeping Jake and off down the embankment towards the river.

Moose wasn't hurt, but he was so startled that he stood upright in his sleeping bag and tent.

So there he was, jumping all around the campsite like a big caterpillar in a cocoon having a one-man sack race shouting, "Whoa - whoa - what happened?"

And I was laughing so hard I couldn't tell him!

But the day doesn't end there. Later, after we cooked breakfast and filled our canteens from the greatest spring in northeast Iowa, we split up and hit the river. By ten o'clock I had caught a couple of nice smallmouth, and had seen a real lunker break water in a large pool. I slowly edged my way out into the head of the pool, which was surrounded by trees and brush on one side and a high cliff on the other. Soon I was in almost to the tops of my hip boots.

I heard someone coming through the brush, and then Jake's voice saying, "Any luck?"

"Mine ain't luck, Old Buddy," I said. "You know that. It's skill. I'm about to demonstrate it by catching a big lunker I spotted here in this pool."

"I'll catch him for you, then," he said, laughing.

I looked around to see him try a backhand horizontal cast with his fly rod, loaded with a Super Duper lure, from under the trees. The move resulted in a horrible miscast, and the lure, instead of dropping in the deeper part of the pool about twenty feet away from me, struck the water about six inches from my right boot. Moose recognized that he had tossed a baddy, so he retrieved the line right away. The retrieving action set the hook in the largest smallmouth either of us had ever seen on the Volga! The bass had taken the lure just as it hit the water, and Jake caught my lunker just six inches from my leg!

The bass jumped, I jumped, my right boot filled with water, and with Moose yelling at me to grab my net, I sat down in about two feet of cold water.

Later, back at the spring, with me dried out before the fire, Jake said, "Bear, I'm going to have that bass mounted."

"The hell you are!" I said. "That's my bass, after what he put me through, I'm going to clean him and fry him for lunch."

And I did, too!

BRIDGE TROUT

Like I said, everything happened to me and Jake—only this time it happened to just him. He was on a combination hunting and fishing trip to Wyoming—without me, dangit—and one morning he woke up real early and couldn't get back to sleep. He just sneaked out quietly to the edge of the cabin camp where he was staying, taking his fly rod. A small wooden bridge crossed a trout stream there, so he proceeded to cast around on both sides of it. Noticing that the best hole seemed to be right under the bridge, Moose, without thinking, dropped his lure right down through a large crack in the floor of the bridge. You guessed it, hooked a very large rainbow!

Then frustration set in. The whole camp was still asleep, and he was too far away to shout loud enough for someone to hear his cries for help. As a last resort, he tied the line to the bridge, then waded up under it in the cold water and grabbed the fish. Luckily it was still on the hook. Jake said it wasn't the biggest trout he had ever caught, by any means —but he had it mounted anyway!

FISHERMAN'S WINE

We were camped on Crane Creek that Labor Day weekend, and had a goodly number of smallmouth and rock bass to our credit. Set up near the truck was our umbrella tent with a canopy, plus a chuck box with a white gas stove to cook on—all the comforts of home for a couple of old fishermen.

We had made camp on Friday evening, then after a good night's sleep and a hearty breakfast, split up and went our separate ways on the stream on Saturday. I came back to the campsite for lunch, as we had agreed to do. While relaxing with a cup of coffee, I spotted Jake coming up the creek bank—and it looked like something was wrong. He wasn't walking too straight, and occasionally he would stumble—falling all the way down once.

He looked at me kind of funny when I offered him a cup of coffee, and without saying a word, entered the tent and flopped down on his sleeping bag, and by the time I made myself some lunch, was snoring loudly.

After I ate my lunch, I picked up my fly rod and trudged off downstream, occasionally flicking a lure into a pool and hooking a nice bass.

About a half mile down, I came to a small washed-out dam, and sitting on it was an older man in bib overalls still-fishing in the pool below it. I joined him.

"Want a drink of wine? I made it myself from rhubarb," he said. "We call it piestengel."

I knew about piestengel, made some myself.

As I lifted the gallon jug and took a swig, I noticed that it was about half empty.

"Is that big guy with you?" he asked.

When I told him yes, he said, "That guy sure liked my wine. He drank almost all that's gone out of that jug. Nice guy. Hope to see him again."

"Hide the jug, next time!" I said.

BEAR'S HOLE

There is a place on Bear Creek which Jake named "Bear's Hole." Why? Because I can walk up to it almost any day, anytime of the year, and pull out my limit of trout.

I used to like to think that they named the stream after me, but it's much older than I am.

About "Bear's Hole," it happened years ago, before we knew this particular stream too well.

Now, Jake is an avid trout fisherman, and a good one, much better than me—although I'll never admit it to him. He always seems to have a sensitive touch, and can see or feel the slightest hit on his fly line. He used to always limit out first.

Bear Creek is never too heavily fished because of the difficulty of getting to it. You can walk a half-mile over a bluff that is as steep as a cow's face, or down a logging road for a mile that is too rough for a mule—or you can walk in level for two miles and wade the creek several times at the lower end where it is deep and cold. This eliminates the lazy type of trout fishermen.

Moose had stopped at the first likely looking hole, and I told him I was going further. Arriving at a good-looking spot with a big rock overhang, and other large rocks out in the creek, I made a cast and immediately caught a fifteen inch rainbow. Then another, and another, and so it went.

Jake showed up a little later empty handed, unusual for him.

Seeing my stringer, which I had not as yet put in my creel, he said, "Those look a little better than the usual, Bear."

"Not bad," I said, as I hauled in another.

I followed him up the creek, and soon found myself one over the limit. As we headed back, him with an empty creel, I asked him to carry my extra.

As we hiked down past my lucrative hole, I told him he ought to throw in there.

He said, "No, I won't fish in Bear's Hole."

And he never has!

Nearing my pickup truck, I said, "Well, Moose, for a highly competitive fisherman, you are taking this remarkably well."

"That's just on the outside!" he growled.

FISHERMAN FOOD

Trout fishermen will eat anything—anything that doesn't try to eat them first—and even some of those things!

There are two kinds of hunters and fishermen—those whose work is primarily inside and who just like to get out, and those who have a definite taste for wild game and fish, and who are meat hunters. Sometimes one is a combination of both.

In winter the hunting and fishing can sort of bog down, but it doesn't need to. Rabbit and coon seasons run late, and some seasons, like coyote, last all year long—depending on where you are.

Ice fishing is getting to be more and more of a popular wintertime sport. It's tougher nowadays, since you can't abandon your tip-up, retire to shore and check it occasionally with binoculars, as you once could. Now you have to stay right with it.

I still like to get out in winter. But, even though when a nice spring day rolls around and I wish I was back on the farm or working as a telephone lineman or something, when the freezing rain and snow arrives I'm glad to be shuffling papers, writing articles and books, and conducting a lot of business by telephone or internet—inside, where I can control the climate.

As for winter fishing, I still like to go after trout in cold weather—where the streams run too fast to freeze.

Not too long ago me and Jake were "enjoying" the fishing of Bloody Run. It rained overnight, the ground thawed, my panel truck, in which we had slept, had sunk to the axles. We built a fire under an overhanging cliff and proceeded to cook up a couple of messes of our "fisherman's specials"—ham chunks, onions, potatoes and eggs, all scrambled and fried up together. There we stood, eating out of our mess kits, as the freezing rain ran off the cliff and fell into our food, making little spewing sounds as it hit the hot pans.

"Boy, that sure goes down good!" I said.

"Yeah," the Moose said, "but if Bettie ever served me up anything like this, I'd beat hell out of her!"

Yes, sir, there is a lot of enjoyment in wintertime fishing!

TROUT, SQUIRRELS AND CATFISH

But it wasn't winter when we had the next set of adventures. It was September, on the Turkey River.

We were tent camping again, and the trout fishing had been reasonably good, when we met The Couple. They were wearing the latest, not to mention the ultimate, in waders, vests, hats and shirts—and were carrying the most expensive looking flyrods we had ever seen, plus nets and bait boxes. They looked like they had just stepped out of Abercrombie and Fitch. Our conversation with them revealed that they had gone on a guided trout fishing expedition in the Rockies, and decided it was their sport—so were trying it here.

"But there are no fish in this stream," she said. "We haven't even had one bite. You men are wasting your time."

Me and Jake looked at each other and grinned. We didn't have the heart to tell them about the five trout we had between us so far, and expected five more—a limit for each of us.

We went up to our tent and tried to take a nap, but kept being interrupted by a large, noisy gray squirrel chattering in a nearby tree. Jake finally got enough of his incessant screeching, and stepped out of the tent and threw a rock at him to chase him away.

We were both surprised when the little timber rodent fell out of the tree, dead, from a blow to the head.

"What are you going to do now?" I asked.

"Let's eat him for supper," said Moose. "Squirrel season is open, and I do have a hunting license. My methods might be a little old fashioned, but I'm legal."

So we did—stewed squirrel and fried trout made a wonderful supper for two tired and hungry outdoorsmen.

Later, at one of our favorite holes, Jake hooked onto something big. It didn't fight like a trout, and besides, there wouldn't be one that big in that river anyway.

When he finally got it up near shore, at the risk of breaking his flyrod, it turned out to be a channel cat—a big one!

"It'll go five pounds, Bear," he said.

"Naw," I said. "You're dreaming."

"Betcha five bucks!"

"You're on!" I said. "Be prepared to pay up."

We stopped at a grocery store in Elkader, and while the clerk was weighing the fish, a lead sinker fell out of its mouth!

"Well, I'll be darned," said the Moose. "It looks like somebody else caught him before me!"

I took the fish away from the clerk, held it up by its tail and shook it. A half- pound of lead fell out on the scale!

"Why, that old cat must like to eat sinkers," said Jake.

"Yeah, sure."

And you know what? That catfish weighed five and a half pounds without the lead—and the Moose was miffed at me because I wouldn't pay off the bet!

GIFTS

Me and Jake figured out how to get what we want for Christmas, and we are more than willing to pass the information on to you as good advice,

When Christmas comes up, some of you woods and waters types are sure to receive sporting goods as gifts. Then again, maybe you won't. Have you tried dropping hints to your wife about that new Remington automatic, or that fiberglass bow? It doesn't work—believe me! She won't know what you are talking about, anyway.

No, that's not the way to do it—never try hinting at your wife, kids or other family members.

Try hinting at your sportsmen friends instead!

Now, those friends aren't going to get you anything for Christmas—especially not a Remington automatic. (Well, one of them might, especially if you give him a twenty-five horse outboard for his birthday.) But they will get the message to your wife.

I first found out about this several years ago when my son and I lost all our fishing gear in a whitewater canoe accident. I just about quit fishing. (And if you believe that, I've got some land down in Florida I'd like to talk to you about!)

Then one spring (the first week in May) I had to address a group of engineers in Rochester, Minnesota.

Old Moose said that he had to go to Minneapolis on business so, "Why don't we meet in Rochester and go down into northern Iowa trout fishing for a few days."

I finally agreed to go, after he convinced me I could use his son's flyrod, plus some of Jake's lures.

Then, on my birthday, April 29, what should I get as a gift from Rosemary and the kids but a beautiful fly rod and a carrying case!

Next day at the office, Moose said, "Hey, how do you like the new fly rod?"

How did he know? He picked it out! Rosemary had asked him what I needed in sports equipment, and knowing nothing about fly rods, she had asked him to select it.

"Oh, I didn't really select it," he said. "I picked the one I knew you would want, then I picked one that cost a lot more and one that was much cheaper—knowing that when she went to the store she would get the one in the middle. And she did."

Of course, there are other ways to get sporting goods for Christmas. There is blackmail, there is horsetrading, there is buying it yourself.

Take the latter. I know one guy who bought his wife a size forty-six hunting coat for Christmas. (She weighs 109.) But, then, she bought him an eight-speed blender for the kitchen.

Then I have a very good friend who received the most beautiful gun cabinet I have ever seen. But his wife got a piano! There is an inequity there somewhere—but horsetrading is horsetrading.

As for blackmail, let me tell you how my son obtained his first shotgun.

He was ten years old. Lots of rabbits in a wood patch behind our place. He had been shooting an air rifle for years and was really very good. In my collection of shotguns I had a sixteen gauge bolt action which he really had his eye on. Before Christmas he started in asking for it as a gift. He had fired it a few times before, so one morning I suggested we stroll through the woods and see if he could hit a rabbit.

To make a long story short, he bagged six rabbits in about an hour, and even though I fired three shots, I didn't hit any. Of course, my excuse was that I had to keep an eye on him and his shooting.

On the way back to the house he said, "Hey, Dad, I know you've taught me to tell the truth, but I could say WE got six rabbits without lying, couldn't I?"

He got the shotgun for Christmas!

But the best way is still to let your friends know. (Lately I've seen Rosemary in close conversations with several friends of mine—so I hope everyone got the message.)

I think I made one mistake, though. I suggested that I would never get anyone anything for Christmas that they might buy themselves.

She said, "There isn't anything you wouldn't get for yourself!"

So I might wind up with an empty sock.

Don't forget I told you how to get what you want, but if your friends are too stupid to pass the word along, that's your problem.

HISTORY

Me and Jake used to sit in our old flat bottomed skiff on one of our favorite rivers, when we were young, and watch the airliners fly overhead, and saying how we would like to be in one of them, going somewhere—anywhere, for business or pleasure.

Then three or four decades later, after we had been flying well over a hundred thousand miles each year, and doing business all over the world—and combining hunting and fishing with the business trips—we found ourselves in an airliner looking down on that very same stretch of river.

As we were pointing out the landmarks visible to us at six miles up, I started laughing.

"You thinking what I'm thinking, Bear?" he asked.

"Yeah, Moose," I answered. "History doesn't repeat itself—it reverses itself!"

OUTDOOR PHRASES

Statement: I got it!

Meaning: I know that seven people shot at it but it's really my bird.

Statement: He went behind an obstruction just as I shot.

Meaning: I missed him by a mile, anyway.

Statement: I never bring game home, because my wife doesn't like to fix it.

Meaning: I didn't get anything.

Statement: I raised three big ones to the top of the water.

Meaning: I didn't catch any fish.

Statement: My stringer broke and I lost them all.

Meaning: I didn't catch any fish.

Statement: They just weren't biting today.

Meaning: Everyone was catching fish but me.

Statement: You are fishing in the best spot, that's why you are catching the most fish.

Meaning: But don't ask me to change with you, because you might start catching them here.

Statement: I have decided to become a catch-and-release fisherman.

Meaning: I never catch anything anyway, and this way I won't be expected to bring anything home.

THE END

www.ingramcontent.com/pod-product-compliance
Ingram Content Group UK Ltd.
Pitfield, Milton Keynes, MK11 3LW, UK
UKHW041914190726
13854UKWH00003B/1249